LET'S GO TO THE
PLAYGROUND

WRITTEN & ILLUSTRATED BY
RUTH WALTON

W

FRANKLIN WATTS
LONDON•SYDNEY

At the weekend we go to the park.
In the park there is a playground with
lots of fun things to do!

You pull the gate open to
enter the playground.

There is a roundabout, a see-saw, rockers, swings and a slide.

What do you like playing on the most?

You push the roundabout to make it spin around.

Going down the slide is great fun!

Do you know how a slide works?

After you've climbed up the ladder, a **force** called **gravity** pulls you down the slide. A force is a push or a pull.

How can you go faster down a slide?

The main force that pulls you down a slide is gravity. Without gravity, we would float up into the air! The thing that slows you down on a slide is another force called **friction**. This happens when two surfaces rub against each other. If you wear clothes made of smooth or shiny material, there will be less friction between your clothes and the smooth metal of the slide.
You will whizz down the slide even faster!

Invisible gravity pulls objects together. On Earth, it pulls everything down towards the ground.

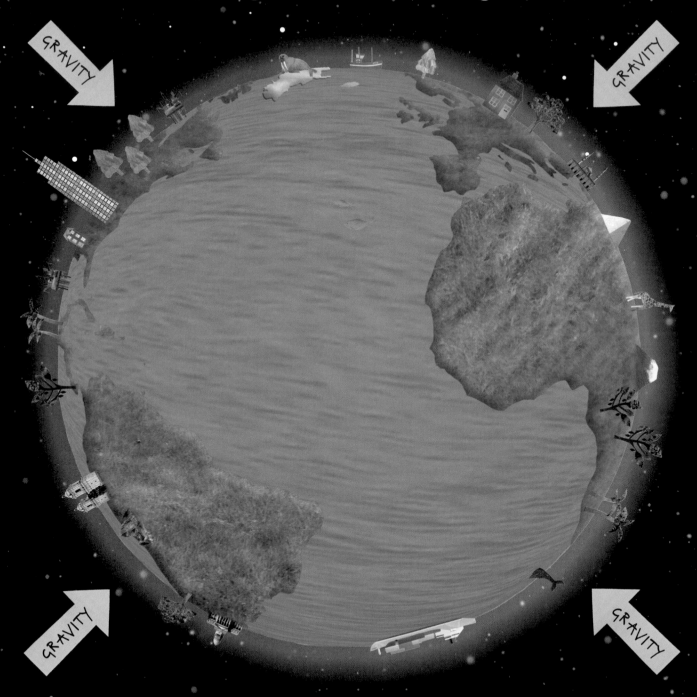

Gravity gives things **weight** and stops everything from drifting off into space.

EXPERIMENT: How does gravity affect moving objects?

What you will need:

Two matching balls

Two people

STEP 1: Find a large flat patch of ground such as a playground or sports field. Look at the diagram below: one of you will drop a ball, and one will throw a ball. You should both let go of the balls from the same height.

STEP 2: After a count of three, let go of the balls. Call out as soon as your ball hits the ground. Try this out a few times, and then swap tasks. Which ball lands first or do they take a similar amount of time?

Person 1

AGREED HEIGHT

Person 2

What have you learned about gravity?

Check your answers on page 29.

This little girl is playing on the see-saw with her brother. They find it easy to lift each other up into the air on the see-saw.

Why do you think this happens?

A see-saw is a type of **lever**.
Each child's weight makes the see-saw tilt up and down on a fixed point, called a **fulcrum**.

Have a good look at the see-saw.

Where do you think the fulcrum is?

All of these things use levers to help them work:

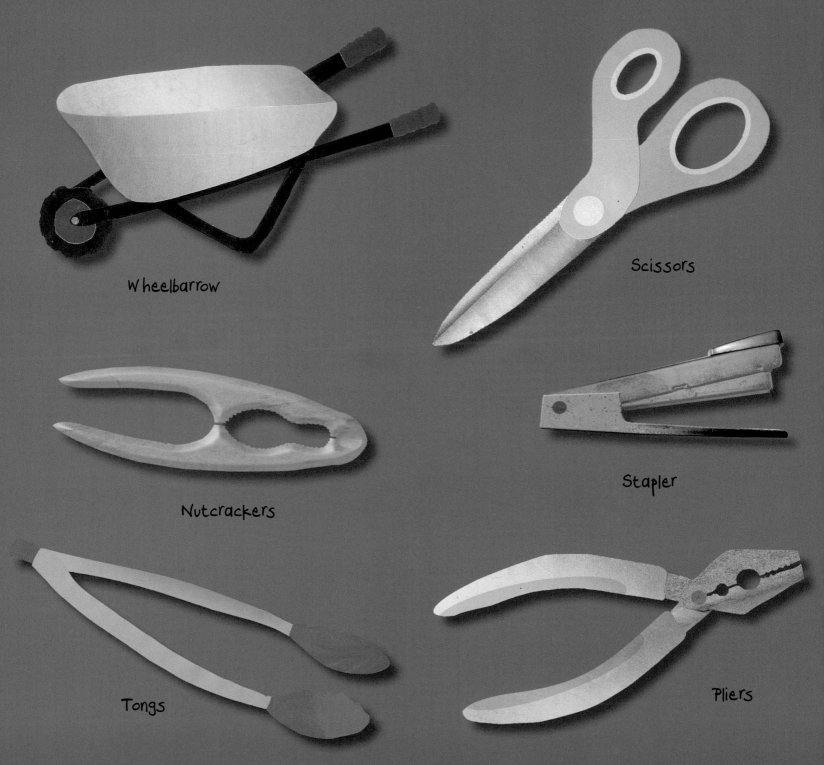

Wheelbarrow

Scissors

Nutcrackers

Stapler

Tongs

Pliers

Which picture is the odd one out and why?

Find the answer on page 29.

At the barbecue

Looking at a map

cutting paper

On the farm

How do swings work?

A swing is a type of **pendulum**. The swing hangs from the frame and can move freely backwards and forwards.

Try sticking your legs out while you are swinging. What happens?

What else can pendulums be used for?

Some clocks use pendulums to keep the time, because each swing of the pendulum takes the same amount of time.

Until the 1930s most clocks had a pendulum, which would swing back and forth, making a 'tick-tock' sound!

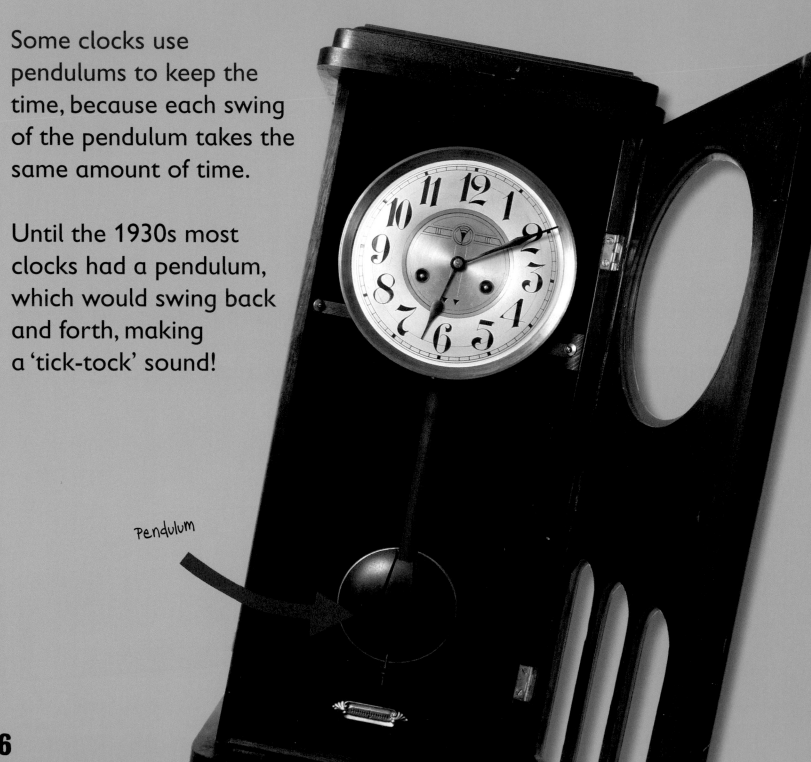

Pendulum

EXPERIMENT: Make a pendulum!

What you will need:

 Metal nuts

 String

 Sticky tape

Stopwatch

A table

STEP 1: Tie the metal nut onto the end of the string. Make a double knot to hold it in place. Attach the other end of the string to the edge of the table using the sticky tape.

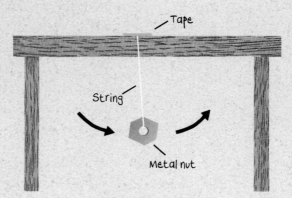

Tape

String

Metal nut

STEP 2: Holding the nut, let go of the pendulum at the level of the table top. At the same time start the stopwatch. Count the number of swings back and forth that the pendulum makes in 30 seconds. Now try timing the swings again, but just give the pendulum a tiny push. Write down your answers.

STEP 3: Add another metal nut and try the experiment again. Does this change the number of swings you can count in 30 seconds? Try changing the length of the string, too! Write down all of the results.

What have you found out?

Check your results on page 29.

If you like to spin around, it's fun to go on the roundabout. When you are spinning around it can feel like something wants you to fly off! This is called **centrifugal force** and it works on objects which are **rotating**.

You can go really fast if you get someone to push it for you, but ask them to stop if you are getting too dizzy!

Why does spinning around make you dizzy?

When you get dizzy it is because your brain is confused by the messages from your body. Your body detects motion using an amazing system inside your ear. Fluid inside one part of your ear touches **nerves** which send messages to your brain. When you spin around, it muddles up the messages, so your body feels like it is still moving even when it has stopped!

Inner ear

If you're feeling dizzy, it's good to lie down until you feel better!

At a fairground, riders on the **carousel** are pushed outwards by centrifugal force.

Have you ever been on a carousel?

Riding a carousel.

Don't forget your seatbelt!

When you are in a car and it goes around a corner, you lean over the other way.

What force makes you lean over?

Check your answer on page 29.

EXPERIMENT: Turn a cup of water upside-down without spilling it!

What you will need:

70cm string

Scissors

Paper cup

Water

STEP 1: Make two holes in opposite sides of the rim of the paper cup, using the scissors. Thread the string through the holes and tie the ends together with a strong knot.

STEP 2: Hold the cup in one hand and give the string a pull to make sure it is secure. Half fill the cup with water.

STEP 3: Hold the string tightly on the knot and gently swing the cup to and fro. After a few swings, spin the cup all the way around. Practise this outside first!

What has happened?
Check your results on page 29.

Check your results on page 29.

Sometimes we go to an adventure playground.
It is very big and it has a wooden frame. There
are lots of different things to play on.

Which force is slowing down this zip-wire?

What is the force that helps a slide work?

Have a good look at the adventure playground and try to answer all of the questions! If you get stuck, look back through the book.

Where can you find a pendulum and a lever?

Where is the fulcrum on this see-saw?

You don't need a playground to play games!
Ball games and other sports are great fun and
good for keeping you fit.

Hula hoops use
centrifugal force!

The girl's foot pushed the
football into the air. Gravity
will bring it back to the
ground again.

Imaginary games are good for your brain and they can be exciting to play.

I'm pretending to be in a skipping contest!

Walking the dog can be even more fun if you use your imagination!

What is your favourite game to play?

ACTIVITY:
Design a playground!

Here are a few things that you might need to make your own playground design.

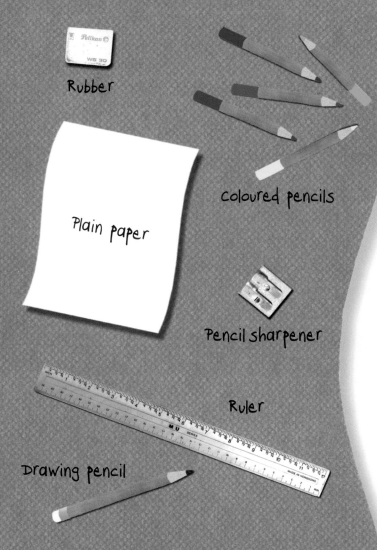

Rubber

coloured pencils

Plain paper

Pencil sharpener

Ruler

Drawing pencil

These pictures may give you some ideas.

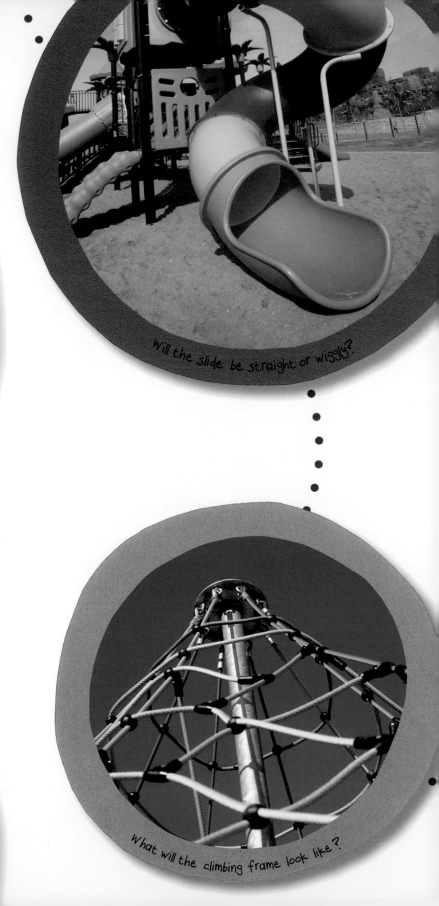

Will the slide be straight or wiggly?

What will the climbing frame look like?

What will you swing on?

Will it have a tree house?

What could you climb on?

Don't worry about your drawing, just have fun.

Use your imagination to design the playground of your dreams!

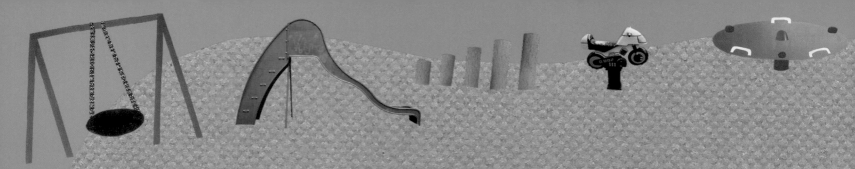

Glossary

Carousel another name for a fairground merry-go-round

Centrifugal force the outward force on a rotating object or person

Force a push or a pull that makes something move, or slow down

Friction the force that slows objects down as they rub against each other

Fulcrum the point on which a lever turns

Gravity the force that gives everything weight and pulls everything towards the ground

Lever a bar or a tool that turns on a fulcrum to lift something or open something

Nerves thin threads that take messages from all parts of your body to the brain

Pendulum a solid object hanging from a fixed point so that it swings freely

Rotating spinning around

Weight how heavy something is

Answers and Results

Page 9: The balls should land at roughly the same time. This shows that gravity affects still and moving objects in the same way!

Page 13: The picture of the children looking at a map is the odd one out. All the others show people using levers.

Page 17: The number of pendulum swings is not affected by its weight or the height of the swing, but it is affected by the length of the string!

Page 20: Centrifugal force pushes your body outwards from the circular movement that the car is making.

Page 21: The water is held in the cup by centrifugal force as it spins around!

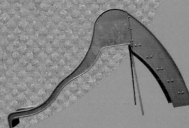

Index

This edition 2012

Franklin Watts
338 Euston Road
London NW1 3BH

Franklin Watts Australia
Level 17/207 Kent Street
Sydney, NSW 2000

Text and illustrations
copyright © Ruth Walton 2011

Series editor: Sarah Peutrill
Art director: Jonathan Hair
Photographs: Ruth Walton, unless
otherwise credited

Dewey number: 796.06'8
ISBN: 978 1 4451 0648 9
Printed in China

Franklin Watts is a division of
Hachette Children's Books, an
Hachette UK company.
www.hachette.co.uk

Picture credits: with thanks to
istockphoto and shutterstock images.